A BEGINNER'S GUIDE TO STOCKS & SHARES

Harding Udoh

HOW TO MAKE MONEY FROM THE STOCK MARKET

Beginners Guide to Stocks & Shares

Published by Morlight International:

+234 7034486687, +234 9065905636

enquiries@morlightng.org, harding625@gmail.com

ISBN: 9798616875655

ASIN: B0851TFLJ7

Cover and interior design: Divi Host & Molodav Prints

International purchase available from www.amazon.com and other leading online book retailers

This book is the first in a series written as a contribution to realizing sections 1, 4, & 10 of the Sustainable Development Goals on the; eradication of Poverty, obtaining a good quality education, and reducing inequalities. Indeed, it is only through proper and timely education of the mind that the equitable distribution of wealth can be achieved.

Contents

NOTES FROM THE AUTHOR

I recall a conversation that took place between my mum and me, decades ago; this was about the time I was to graduate from university. During this conversation, she drew my attention to understand what shares are and the potential they could play in helping me grow wealth. My mum is an educationist and one given to career, and I believe that somewhere along her career path while trying to multiply her earnings, she came across the concept of share investing. She stressed the need to start out investing early buying shares once I began earning. As loving as this advice was, I thought I got the gist of what she tried to teach, but alas, I had not grasped a tenth of it. All that registered to me at the time were the words "ensure you buy shares as soon as you start earning." I did listen and heard all she had to say, but it was not alive in me.

Like most youngsters who learned from seeing things done, I took in her words, albeit in a shallow manner, for upon graduating, I only nursed the desire to secure a job and just as she did build a career.

Two decades later, having experienced the ins and outs of following a career path, I have found that the need to build and sustain wealth has far outlived the desire to solely pursue a career and climb to the top of this ladder. I know a lot better now that it is not so much about the number of jobs you get during your climb in career, but actually what you do with what you have achieved and earned while on those jobs.

Through self-study and trading in stocks, I have brought to life what my mother tried to give to me in a few sentences. Somehow, in the hustle and bustle of tending a regular job, I did buy into the stocks of a few reliable companies in Nigeria that over, the years, have outperformed the market.

Do note my words "buy into," because at the time, I was not awake to terms such as: **"stock markets," Public Offer," "Investing,"** and **"Trading."** I had all but forgotten about these investments if not for the regular receipt of; dividend warrants and letters informing of bonus shares. Surprisingly, as I held onto these shares the amounts used in buying them had grown by a little more than 250% over the years (via bonus shares, dividend, and capital appreciation), I had no clue of their growth at the time.

At the time of my investing in those shares, the process of buying into them was entirely manual. Most individuals that traded then were either senior citizens, retirees, or stockbrokers. Today technological advancement has made things seamless. Competition between investment houses has also led to lower transaction costs and lowered the barriers of entry to foster financial inclusion, thereby making the market more liquid.

Today I practically sit in front of my computer or make use of my mobile phone to buy or sell shares on my own without needing the physical intervention of a stockbroker to help fulfill my trading activities. Not only do I now invest in stocks, but I trade in them as well, maintaining a personal capital appreciation of between 20 to 30% per trade.

Looking back, I realize that I could have adopted this mode of investing as a hobby alongside my jobs, spending just about an hour per week with excellent results. I could have consciously and actively grown wealth using this investment vehicle monthly if I had early exposure to mentorship and useful books on investing which painstakingly explained to me what shares were, what the stock market was, how to access it, how I could grow wealth through them and what pitfalls to avoid.

It is this early opportunity and exposure to stocks which I missed while younger that has provided the drive to share my experience with young people while at the same time attempting to use this book to help furnish them with the necessary information and exposure required to invest comfortably in or trade shares

Harding Udoh

January 2020.

CHAPTER 1: INTRODUCTION

Once upon a time, when you asked working-class people if they ever considered investing in shares or the stock market and what their views about shares were, the majority of responses would not have been very far from the following reactions; "yes, I have but do not know much about it and how to invest in them," "I do not consider it to be a safe investment vehicle or a viable option for growing their money." Otherwise, some saw it as an easy way to lose one's life's savings.

Indeed, as recently as the mid-1990s, only about one-tenth of Nigerian adults stood invested in the stock market, and the descriptions of some individuals associated with share ownership were those that depicted market tragedies, with stock market analysts lending a voice to the latest bad to worsening news of the market.

Thankfully, these illustrations, while true in some cases, bear no resemblance to the entirety of the market experience of most shareholders – that is assuming that they approached the market with a mid to long term view of reliable companies. Like most other mainstream investment vehicles (property, cash, and fixed income) over time, shares have produced considerably healthy returns – despite the occasional market reversals.

Today it is pleasing to see more and more people investing in shares. Share ownership among young Nigerians is also on a steady increase, either directly or indirectly, through managed mutual funds. This improvement is made possible by the advent of technology and also partly due to a rise in digital platforms and marketing efforts to enlighten investors of the opportunities that lay with investing in stocks.

INVESTMENT TIP 1: Never invest in anything that you do not understand. Endeavor to carry out your research first before investing.

CHAPTER 2: WHAT ARE SHARES?

Shares also widely referred to as "stocks" or "equities" are most times used interchangeably.

Shares for this book can be defined as representing part ownership of a company. When you buy shares in a company, you invariably become a part-owner of that company. You take ownership or take up equity in it. Which is why shares are also referred to as "equities." At times shares are referred to as "stock."

Companies will offer their shares to the public in a bid to raise funds. Funds raised can be used for a variety of purposes, but typically used to finance operations and the expansion of existing business, establishing a new venture, or funding company takeovers.

Whenever the shares of a company are being offered to the public, this event is known as a "Public Offer" or "float." First-time offers are referred to as an "IPO," meaning "Initial Public Offer." Subsequent share offerings from the same company are then generally referred to as "Public Offer" or "Share Issues."

As a shareholder, it is important to bear in mind that in taking up the shares of a company, you are participating in both the good and bad fortunes of the companies in which you have invested. If the company performs well, you benefit from high share prices and healthy dividends. Should the company operate at a loss either as a result of poor corporate governance or economic hardships stemming from unfavorable government policies, then you will also share in the misfortunes. The one thing you, fortunately, don't partake of as a shareholder, is a company's indebtedness. Implying that if a company collapses leaving behind debts, as a shareholder, you are not responsible for paying the debt. As such, the most that you stand to lose as a shareholder is the amount of money; you paid to acquire the shares.

INVESTMENT TIP 2: Learn to pay yourself first. Do not be lulled into believing that 100% of your earnings are yours alone. Often, we tend to live under the illusion that all we earn belong solely to us. Somehow, we forget; the lineup of those who almost daily collect a share of our well-earned pay; the transport service, the phone service, the taxman, the fast-food provider, home maintenances…do not wait until there is nothing left to save.

CHAPTER 3: HOW COULD MONEY BE MADE FROM INVESTING IN SHARES?

There are three ways to make money by investing in shares, namely;

1. Capital growth
2. Dividend yield
3. Bonus shares and discounted rights issues

Firstly, you can make money from share price increase or price appreciation. Implying that you would realize a profit from **capital growth**, once there is an increase in the price of shares.

Secondly, you can make money through **dividend yields**, resulting from profit distribution made by companies after the end of a financial year if the company's performance is favorable

Thirdly but less frequently, you can also make money from the occasional receipt of freely declared **bonus shares** and the purchase of **discounted "rights issues."**

CAPITAL GROWTH

Capital growth occurs when the trading price of the company's shares appreciates or rises, reflecting the company's positive performance, and good future outlook, which means that the company experienced a favorable economic environment during the period. So, if for example, you buy a stock valued at N2 per share, and a few weeks or months after, the company's share traded price rises to N4 per share; it means that you have effectively doubled the value of your investment. However, should the share price fall to N1, you would have lost half of your invested capital due to the decrease in price. It is that simple.

A degree of capital growth or appreciation can also occur through taking advantage of **"rights issues,"** which is usually offered at a discounted price from the prevailing market price. A rights issue occurs when a company is attempting to raise more capital for its business, invites existing shareholders to buy additional shares at a discounted rate to the current market price. This discounted value acts as an incentive for the shareholder to take up the offer. The new number of new shares the shareholder is invited to buy is always proportional to the existing number of shares that the shareholder already holds.

Although opportunities to take up the right issues do not happen all the time, it will typically require an additional outlay of funds to exercise the right or to benefit from the arrangement.

As an example, let's say Company A was trading at N5 per share. It then offers its shareholder one new share at N4.50 for every five shares held, representing a discounted price of 50 kobos or 10%. If you were to buy into the offer, you would be paying 50k less per share than you would have paid if there were no rights issue opportunities for that share. If you have bought into the rights issue and then decided to sell the shares soon, you would have realized a capital appreciation on your investment, which would likely be selling at a higher price than you paid for to secure your stake in the rights issue.

DIVIDENDS

If the listed company in which you own shares makes a profit, as a part-owner of the company, you are entitled to share in the profits as declared at an Annual General Meeting. The company distributes these profits as deemed reasonable and approved by the directors, in the form of what is called a "**dividend**," which is typically paid out every six or twelve months.

The size of the dividend (a portion of the profit-sharing coming to you) depends on how many of the company's shares you own and what proportion of the company's profits the directors have chosen to distribute to shareholders.

INVESTMENT TIP 3: Be deliberate! To grow wealth, you must be as focused as you would be on a career.

CHAPTER 4: WHAT SORT OF RETURNS CAN I EXPECT TO MAKE BY INVESTING IN SHARES?

Many studies carried out on the Nigerian and overseas share markets have illustrated just how attractive investment in shares can be.

A look at the performance of shares in Nigeria from data culled from the Nigerian Stock Exchange shows that the most common annual returns by percentage in **blue-chip companies** were in a range of between 15 to 50%. At the extreme, a negative -50 to -20% occurred, while the best returns of between 60 to 120% cumulative return on investment could be achieved in some years when you consider capital appreciation, dividends, and assuming the reinvestment of all dividends.

WHAT TO KNOW ABOUT PRICE VOLATILITY

It is important to note that the returns you get from shares are neither fixed nor guaranteed. Just as the fortunes of the company you invest in can rise and fall, so too can the value of your stocks and the returns you earn from them rise or fall.

These ups and down movement in the prices of shares is called "**volatility**." While some share prices can be more volatile than others, it is just this volatility that is responsible for making shares a better investment over the long term than the short term. The longer shares are held on to, the more the highs and lows attain to the equilibrium price and are balanced out.

SHARES VS OTHER INVESTMENTS

Shares have been known to have some compelling advantages over other mainstream asset classes because stocks generally provide better long-term returns than other comparable mainstream assets and are a good hedge against value eroding inflation.

In addition to worthwhile returns, there are other reasons why shares make an excellent long-term investment vehicle; these reasons include the facts that;

- Stocks are highly **"liquid,"** meaning they can be sold and converted very quickly to cash. As such, you are not locked in by your investment for prolonged time frames. Also, unlike rental properties, you can sell units of shares rather than having to sell-off the entire investment

- The market value of shares can be determined on any given trading day only by looking up the share price listing on the stock exchanges, daily newspapers, or by listening to market news. The market value of an investment property, on the other hand, is highly subjective, with the range of valuations limited only by the number of agents engaged

- One of the big attractions of shares is that you can achieve a high degree of diversification, thereby considerably reducing the level of risk exposure. For example, spreading a N10,000 investment across five different top-performing companies, assuming one buys minimum share units of N2000 in each company. Also, investing in a managed share fund will give you access to averagely about 30 companies in a range of markets. Meanwhile, investing similar amounts directly in real estate (hypothetically speaking) would give you a deposit on a single property

- While it is nice to cast an eye over your investment property with the inner satisfaction of ownership, it's not such a beautiful perspective when your returns are whittled away by repair and maintenance costs, when you have to attend court summonings to evict tenants from the building, or when the property remains untenanted for months. On the other hand, shares in profitable companies don't require any further input or labor from you

- The barrier costs for entry and exit into the share market are quite low. Even though it is inevitable that some transaction costs associated with share purchase or sale are to be incurred (notably brokerage fees), these are quite negligible when compared to the legal costs, stamp duties, and agency fees associated with a property.

INVESTMENT TIP 4: Avoid leaving money in low-interest bank accounts as the future value of such funds will not be much different ten years from now. If, however, you put such funds into the shares of a good company, the value of the monies could have appreciated by over 100% over the same period.

CHAPTER 5: UNDERSTANDING THE STOCK MARKET

In previous chapters we have considered what a share is, how money is to be made from stocks, and how shares could perform over time, it is now time to for us to examine the share market itself. How does the share market operate, who are its participants, and how is it to be accessed and used?

Today, most countries have their Stock Market, which, due to advances in technology, are now entirely computerized, highly regulated, and effectively operated as marketplaces where shares are listed, to be bought and sold. Each of these listed companies varies in size and may be categorized as a small, medium, or large capitalized company (depending on the size of their capitalization).

All companies, as a rule, must be registered with the Corporate Affairs Commission before operations but do not have to be listed on the stock exchange. To have companies listed on the Stock Exchange, they must apply and, at a certain point in their development, may take this route, although a vast majority do not. The incentive for listing is that it enables companies to raise funds through the sale of their shares and other financial instruments on the Stock Exchange.

Conditions for listing on an Exchange varies from one country to the next. However, generally, a company has to have attained a specific size in; assets, worth at least a stipulated amount in pre-tax profits, have shares freely available for trading; and must meet the local stock exchange listing requirements for financial reporting and disclosure of crucial information. All these regulations are placed to keep would-be fraudsters out of the market, thereby serving to protect shareholders from losing their investments.

TYPES OF MARKET (PRIMARY VS SECONDARY MARKET)

It is crucial to know the difference between the primary and secondary stock markets. When a company issues stock for the first time and sells them directly to investors, this occurs on the **PRIMARY MARKET**.

During an IPO, a primary market transaction takes place between the purchasing investor and the investment bank underwriting the IPO. Any proceeds from the sale of shares on the primary market go to the company that issued the stock.

If these initial investors decide to sell their shares in the company, they will do so on the **SECONDARY MARKET**. Transactions on this market occur between investors only, and the earnings of each sale go to the selling investor.

Primary market prices are set beforehand, while forces of demand and supply determine prices in the secondary market. If investors believe a stock will increase in value and hasten to buy it, the stock price will rise. If a company, on the other hand, loses preference with investors or fails to post positive earnings, its stock price will decline as demand for it shrinks.

The secondary market is a market where investors buy and sell stocks that are already owned. It is a trading arrangement that facilitates the purchase of securities or assets from other investors rather than from issuing companies. The Nigerian Stock Exchange is an example of such markets.

Trades that occur on the secondary market are described as such simply because they are a further step away from the deal that created the securities.

Overall in secondary markets, investors exchange with each other rather than the issuing entity. Also, the secondary market through succession or series of independent yet interconnected trades drives the price of securities towards their actual value through the interplay of demand and supply.

INVESTMENT TIP 5: Learn to distinguish needs from wants. A need is something vital for survival; if not met, it will lead to the onset of disease, inability to function effectively in society, or even death. Anything outside these is a want.

CHAPTER 6: BUYING AND SELLING OF SHARES?

As earlier stated, you can buy and sell shares directly from an Issuing House during a company's Initial Public Offer or on the Secondary Market by opening an account with an approved stock broking house or dealer. A majority of these houses or stockbrokers now have an online presence, so you can sit in front of your computer or from the tab of your phone to perform transactions on their platform once you registered with them as a customer.

Before we proceed further, let's try to understand a few terminologies, which you will come across as you deepen your knowledge of investing:

1. **IPO (Initial Public Offer):** this happens in the primary market when a company floats or lists shares of the very first time. The company goes to raise money from the members of the public by having its shares listed on the stock market for the first time. The new shares are offered to the public at a set price per share in specific share-unit sizes. To buy into an IPO, you fill out the application form in the prospectus – circulated by brokers or appointed agents. After

completing the form with your necessary information then it is to be submitted along with your cheque for the units subscribed, either to the company directly, or to its agents. On the other hand, where the IPO is by listing on the stock exchange, you buy through a broker.

2. **Secondary Market:** this is where buying and selling of existing shares take place. When you want to buy stocks that have already been issued in the market and are now being transferred from one buyer to the other, you get such deals on the secondary market. These types of shares that are not obtained through an IPO will typically be trading on the share market. Here, you only have one way of doing it, which is through a stockbroker or firm that has a stockbroking license. When you wish to sell the shares purchased, you use the same route as to when buying shares through a stockbroker.

CHOOSE A REPUTABLE STOCKBROKER

Choosing a stockbroker is not such a difficult task. I categorically suggest that you do this by way of referral. You may consider asking family members, friends, or colleagues to recommend one or visit your country's stock exchange website as it usually hosts a contact list of all registered stockbrokers and investment houses in the country.

You should look to engage the services of a Stock Broking Firm with:

- Record transaction volumes
- Excellent after-sales investor support and care
- Regular provision of market research, recommendations, and investor advice
- Straight through online transaction processing service
- Competitive service costs

It is imperative to note the distinction between full-service brokers and discount brokers or dealers when selecting a service provider.

FULL-SERVICE BROKERS VS DISCOUNT BROKERS

In keeping with other areas of the financial world, competition in the broking business has been on a steady increase. So, a significant decision you will have to make is that of which type of broker to choose, **full service or discount?**

Generally, a full-service broker should provide you with the following:

1. Personalized services
2. Tailored advice on which shares to buy and sell
3. Access to Venture Capitalist and Private Placement opportunities
4. Access to other investments, including options, debentures, and bonds
5. Tax advice

With these services, you will pay for additional levels of care, consultation, or service. Full-service brokerage fees usually hover between 1 to 2% of the total amount of your transaction.

Alternatively, discount brokers majority of which are online, offer a one size fits all kind of service; this is done to carry out your trades cheaply. They leverage heavily upon technology for effective market penetration. They rarely (if at all) provide personal advice on which shares to buy or sell but offer discounted brokerage rates of around 0.1% or less than what full-service brokers charge.

Furthermore, online brokers provide you with access to your portfolio 24 hours a day, and you can trade from wherever you are, so long as you have an active internet connection regardless of device and location.

The challenge for some individuals, however, is that using an online discount broker requires you doing your research. These days several online brokers provide investment research, but the information provided is only as useful as your understanding of it. Remember Information is not the same as advice, particularly when data is circulated generally.

Both full service and online discount brokers have their fair share of challenges. On the one hand, full-service brokers have been accused of advising clients to buy or sell selfishly to generate fees. Others have recommended investments offering dull returns to investors, but high commissions for the broker. Conversely, investors using online brokers have encountered clogged servers during high market volatility, lengthy hold-ups on customer service lines, and, at times, missed orders.

Should you take the online route, look to choose a broker that offers **"straight-through processing."** **(STP)**. STP refers to a fully automated system where your placed orders travel directly from your computer to the Stock Exchange Automated Trading System, usually taking around ten to fifteen seconds. It is vital in today's trading as some brokers still make use of manual systems where staff read your order from the Internet and place it manually into their system, taking considerably longer times and could cost you more during times when high volumes are traded and are error-prone. Do not forget to ask, should this not be mentioned on the brokers' website.

If you decide to make use of a full-service broker, ask for a commission schedule that spells out the fees, you will be charged, and always ask why a particular financial product is being recommended to you, as your broker will earn more commissions on some products than on others.

So which type of broker should you use? If you have the time and interest to do your research and are confident about making your own decisions, a discount broker is excellent. But for first-time investors, it is probably not a bad idea to consider using a full-service broker until such a time that you may have obtained a reasonable grasp of how the share market works to avoid losing money to ignorance of market activities.

ACCOUNT OPENING REQUIREMENTS

Today opening a stockbroking account can be fully achieved online as most brokers leverage technological advancement to penetrate the market while at the same time providing exceptional and seamless service to potential and existing investors. Most brokers will require the following information in line with Know Your Customer **(KYC)** regulatory policies. So, you will need to provide these by uploading the under listed to open an account:

- Fully completed online account opening form
- Valid means of identity; most brokers will require that you submit either a clear image of your National Driver's License, International Passport, National Identity Card or National Voters Card
- Passport photograph
- Valid Utility Bill

- Banking details; including Bank Verification Number, Bank name and account number

PLACING ORDERS TO BUY OR SELL SHARES

After selecting a broker and opening a stockbroking account, a clearing-house number is assigned to you at the central securities clearinghouse. This account can be likened to a bank account but utilized strictly for recording and tracking the buying and selling of shares traceable to you.

As most brokers have automated their share buy or sell processes, most of these go straight through to the exchange. However, these fundamentally work in the way described below;

When you issue an instruction to your stockbroker to buy or sell shares on your behalf, you could request them to act in one of two ways.

One is to place a **"limit order,"** where you set the highest price you are willing to buy at **(bid price)** and the lowest price you are ready to sell **(offer price)**. Under these instructions, your broker will only act within your set limits.

On the other hand, you can place a **"market order,"** which instructs your broker to fulfill your order at the best price they can under the prevailing market conditions.

From experience, I recommend that you always issue limit order instructions to safeguard your capital as best as possible from exorbitantly priced shares or unattractive share prices.

INVESTMENT TIP 6: A want is anything desired, which is not extremely necessary for survival. Overspending on such desires erodes the potential to build wealth.

CHAPTER 7: WHICH SHARES SHOULD I BUY?

So, you have successfully identified a broking firm who is now your service provider, opened a stockbroking account and now want to place an order to buy your first shares. You are now saddled with the question of which share to buy?

It is significant to note that the quality of stocks varies according to the financial performance of the companies that issue them. As such, **"there are shares, and there are shares."** Investing in shares of just any company carries huge risks. However, if you buy a basket of decent stocks and hold on to them for the mid to long-term, you should generate more satisfactory returns with minimal risk.

Shares recommended by professionals and experts are those of well-established and well-managed companies that have an excellent operational track record and good profitability over the years. In other words, the professional will recommend that you invest in **"blue-chip companies "** or **"bellwether stocks"** companies. A bellwether stock is a stock that marked as a leading indicator of the direction of the economy or a sector of the market or the market as a whole. These are typically largely capitalized equities.

When this category of companies report strong earnings, they usually indicate that the economy is strong and vice versa.

Having said this, I have learned from the market and place a percentage of my money not only on this category of companies but also on well-managed, good performing small to medium-sized companies. However, picking the best is not particularly easy.

It is not recommended that you invest in the shares of so-called **"speculative"** ventures, that is, companies which are new and small, and which will no doubt need more than a fair share of good luck to be successful. There are always a few small companies on the share market that fit into this description. They are the ones that will go into profit if they come out successful or hit it big. Regard these sorts of companies as the outsiders in any race, if they hit their target, they will make a fortune, and so will you, but the odds are slim. There is a better chance they will go broke, taking your money with them.

And so how do you choose shares? Unless you are very enthusiastic about researching companies yourself, it is not a bad idea to let a broker make some recommendations to you. Ideally, you should end up with several shares in different sectors. By **"sectors,"** I mean; manufacturing, banking, telecommunications, construction, and so on. Four of my personal favorites in the Nigerian market being: banking, industrial goods, energy, and health. Always bear in mind that to be invested in a range of sectors helps to spread your risk. If you think that achieving this will be difficult for you, then consider investing in a share managed fund that will invariably take care of the share and sector selections for you, thereby providing diversification.

In the section of this book dedicated to further reading, I have recommended the work **"How to Make Money in Stocks (William J. O'Neil)"** this was suggested because of the soundness of advice and strategic guidance William provided the reader.

I have learned the following and adopt them in picking stocks each time I grapple with the question, "which company's stocks do I invest in?" I hope that these very questions will serve to be faithful companions to you each time the need to pick stocks comes to mind, as they have been to me;

- Learn to read and understand the quarterly performance and earnings of the companies you are interested in – the higher, the better

- Look for significant and steady quarterly and annual growth

- Be on the lookout for new management, new products, and unique service announcements

- Look out for significant volume or movement demand for shares

- Always opt to invest or take up shares in leading companies of identified sectors avoiding the laggards

- Look out for institutional buy-ins and cautiously follow the leaders

- Learn to keep up to date with economic headwinds (policy and politics).

INVESTMENT TIP 7: Be deliberate! To grow wealth, you must be as focused as you would be on a career.

CHAPTER 8: INTERPRETING SHARE MOVEMENT TABLES IN THE NEWS AND STOCK EXCHANGES

The daily trading on national exchanges is reported in the business segment of the news and most national newspapers. These share trading tables contain a wealth of information, most of which you will find relevant in building your share portfolio. However, you must understand how to interpret these so that they may be of value to you.

When reviewing share market trading tables in the financial pages of your daily newspaper, you are likely to find the following headings, the knowledge of which will prove useful in your quest to build wealth.

They have been defined here for your reference and use:

- **COMPANY NAME:** the name of the company that has issued the share

- **STOCK EXCHANGE CODE:** the code given by the national stock exchange to every listed company share on issue

- **LAST SALE PRICE:** price at which the LISTED company's shares last traded at

- **+/- (also denoted using green or red up and down arrows):** is the difference (in kobo's or cents) in a shares last traded price as compared to the sales price of the day before. Indicating daily if the share price has risen or fallen in price

- **QUOTE (BUY):** is the highest price that buyers bided for a stock. It is also known as the "bid" or "buying price."

- **QUOTE (SELL):** is the lowest price at which sellers are willing to sell the shares, also known as the "offer price" or "selling price."

- **VOLUME:** is the total number of shares traded in the company on the previous trading day. Indicating the level of the market interest in a stock

- **DAY'S HIGH AND LOW:** gives the range of prices the shares traded between on the exchanges trading day. Indicating volatility of the share price

- **52-WEEK HIGH AND LOW:** lists the highest and lowest price the share has traded for on the stock exchange in the year to date. Some investors look at the current share price and compare it to the 52-week high and low as a guide as to whether to buy, sell or hold onto the share

- **EARNINGS PER SHARE (EPS):** it shows the amount of profit earned for every ordinary issued share. EPS; calculated by dividing the company's net profit by the total number of ordinary issued shares.

- **DIVIDEND PER SHARE (DPS):** is the size of the latest annual dividend distributed by the company per share

- **DIVIDEND TIMES COVERED:** is the number of times the DPS is covered by the earnings per share (EPS). The ratio relates to a company's profit to the amount of the dividend it pays. If a company produces a profit, it doesn't necessarily pay it all back as a dividend, as the company may decide to use some of the profit for finding new markets or developing a new product. The DPS does not reflect this and the number of times the dividend is covered by profit can be a more valid indication of a company's profitability

- **DIVIDEND YIELD (%):** is the dividend return accruing to the shareholder in relation to the last quoted sale price. It is computed by dividing dividends per share with the previous sale price, expressed as a percentage. As a rule, the higher the dividend yield, the healthier the company is perceived to be and the happier its shareholders are likely to be

- **PRICE TO EARNING RATIO (P/E RATIO):** is arrived at by dividing the last sale price by the earnings per share. It measures the share price in relation to the company's profits. This ratio provides a means of measuring investor expectations of the company's performance. If a company has a small P/E ratio compared to other companies working in the same or similar industries, it indicates that the market anticipates a poor profit performance from the company in the future. A relatively high P/E ratio, on the other hand, indicates the opposite view. A high P/E ratio could also indicate a company is being valued for its asset backing and not for its earnings potential

- **PERCENTAGE MOVE:** shows by what percentage the share price has moved and in what direction daily, weekly, monthly, or yearly.

WHAT ABOUT FUTURE PERFORMANCE?

The interpretative ratios, EPS, DPS, P/E, and so on, all offer insightful information. However, because they are based on historical data, the insights they bring to bear on the present and future share performances must be well-thought-out with some amount of caution. This warning applies especially to the P/E ratio to which many investment commentators assign too much significance and emphasis.

Studying and understanding share market performance ratios is useful, but it will not unveil or reveal which shares you should buy, and which are to be avoided.

These ratios provide a way of comparing shares historical performance to that of another. You may use them as guides, but do not rely heavily on them as definitive answers to the fundamental question: WHICH SHARES SHOULD I BUY?

INVESTMENT TIP 8: A diversified portfolio of shares is bound to earn you more money over the long term, as against putting all your eggs in one basket. Do not place all your money on only one company's stock.

CHAPTER 9: SHARE INDICES

Almost daily, we watch and listen to news commentaries describing the movement of share market indices such as the Nigerian ASI (All Share Index), the New York Dow Jones, the London FTSE and the Hong Kong Hang Seng, without really understanding what is being discussed? For many individuals, these indices may pose a mystery, despite the critical role that they play in share investing.

Across the world, Stock Exchanges develop indices to keep an eye on happenings in particular markets and sectors.

Indexes reflect a change in the value of a sample selection of shares in a single market or a collection of markets.

When an index is created, a selected day is assigned a base value (say 1000), and then changes in market direction are measured against that value. Let's assume that market activity was strong over a period, and on this day, and our sample index rose to 1024, this would imply that the value of the sampled market has increased by 2.4%.

Each stock exchange will have a primary index that represents the market. The ones commonly quoted by the media include the: Nigerian All-Share Index (ASI), New York's Dow Jones Industrial Average, London's FTSE 100 Index, Australia's All Ordinaries Index, Tokyo's Nikkei Index, and Hong Kong's Hang Seng Index (internationally).

In addition to these overall market indices, there are also specific market sector indices, such as the Banking Index, Pension Index, etc. which you will find listed in the share pages of the major daily newspapers.

As a recap, let's look at some of the more major global indices:

- **London's FTSE 100:** is the UK equivalent of the Nigerian All-Share Index. It is commonly called the "footsie" and stands for the "Financial Times Stock Exchange Index." The index is based on the weighted average share price of the leading 100 UK listed companies.

- **New York's Dow Jones Industrial Average** is the oldest and most widely quoted indicator of share market change. It is not an index, but rather, it indicates the average share price of a group of 30 blue-chip companies actively traded on the New York Stock Exchange (NYSE), which is the largest in the world.

- **The All Ordinaries Index (the All Ord's):** is the most frequently quoted in the Australian media. It covers the largest 500 companies actively traded on the ASX. The companies are selected according to their market value.

- **The Nikkei 300:** is the market index for the Tokyo Stock Exchange. It reflects the value of 300 of Japan's leading listed companies.

- **The Morgan Stanley Capital International World Index (MSCI World Index):** indicates the average change in share prices in a sample of international share markets. The share prices of over 1500 companies in around twenty different countries are included in the sample, accounting for 60% of the value of the world's shares.

Should you come across an index which is unfamiliar to you, Google to read about it or call up your stockbroker or funds manager who should not have trouble telling you how the index is constructed, what it measures and what it will mean for you.

INVESTMENT TIP 9: Invest in shares over time because they will generate good to outstanding returns. There is no cause to believe this pattern will change in the foreseeable future.

CHAPTER 10: FIVE TIPS TO GET YOU STARTED

1. DO NOT TRY TO TIME THE MARKET:

Lots of financial commentators and investors place great emphasis on timing your entry into and exit out of the market correctly. **"Correct"** timing means buying when the market or a particular share price is at its lowest and selling when the market or a share is at its highest point. Therefore, most people urge you to get your market timing right. Anyone who can succeed in consistently picking share movements will end up becoming very rich. But, selecting and getting your timing right with share markets is easier said than done.

A sobering study on **"active trading"** that is moving in and out of the market in an attempt to catch its optimum times reveals that an active trader would theoretically need to get their timing right about 66% of the time to break even. But when you add brokerage and other costs of share trading, your timing must be right about 70% of the time before the value of your portfolio is increased.

When you consider the vast array of factors that affect businesses and markets, including economic, political, and social events, some of which can be devastating and utterly unpredictable, you begin to appreciate why it's near impossible to forecast price movements accurately over short periods. And pulling out of a market because of short term ups and downs will cost you dearly.

WHEN THEN IS THE RIGHT TIME TO BUY?

The answer to this question is quite simple: when you have the money. If you wait for the market or a particular share to bottom (the best time to buy), you could wait for quite a long time, because there is no way of knowing when the price of a stock or the market has reached its lowest point.

WHEN IS THE RIGHT TIME TO SELL?

Again, the answer to this question is also quite simple: when you need the money. If you do not need the money, don't sell. It is not the best of strategies to turn your shares over too often (that is, trading excessively by buying and selling too regularly). If you do:

- You will incur unnecessary brokerage fees
- You may incur significant capital gains tax
- You may miss out on the payment of dividends
- You may be out of the market during highly profitable periods

In fact, about the only reasonable time to sell is if a company's shares grow actively and in terms of value become too large a growth on your investment portfolio, putting it out of balance with your other stocks and assets. In this situation, you can rebalance your portfolio by selling off some that share. The idea behind this is to maintain good diversification within your portfolio, in an attempt not to allow any one share or asset to dominate it.

2. ALWAYS TAKE A MID TO LONG TERM VIEW

Taking a long-term view is a must and calls for discipline. You should avoid trying to time your entry into and exit from the share market in the hope of gaining a short-term win, they do exist but can be rare. That's the gamblers' strategy, and gamblers usually lose. The sure way to win with shares or any other mainstream investment is to hang on to your placements for the mid to long term, and that means at least three to five years.

If you are not prepared to adopt this approach, you may as well consider taking your savings for a bet. Returns on share investments are near impossible to predict accurately over one or two years. You must look to the mid to long term, meaning at least three years. While the average very long-term return from developed country shares is between 2 to 5%, stocks in the African space are between 15 to over 100%; however, profits can fluctuate from year to year.

It is vital to have in mind that the share market will have its bad days, weeks, and years just as it will have its good turns. This said history has shown us time and again that the markets always recover and even grow to new heights. It has ever done so, and there is no reason to believe that this pattern will change in the foreseeable future. Where you are in doubt, look at the graphic representation of the all-share index of your nation's bourse (stock exchange). You could consider plotting a performance trend of the last five years of stocks on the Exchange; it is sure to present a compelling argument for market play. The longer you hold onto your shares, the more the high and low returns are smoothed out.

3. INVEST REGULARLY

It is rather tricky to pick the best times to invest except in retrospect because the market is continuously being traded in. By using a strategy popularly known as **"Dollar-cost averaging,"** you do not have to try to pick the optimum times to enter and exit the markets. Dollar-cost averaging involves investing an amount of money at a set frequency into the share market. It is a different approach from active trading, and it causes you to purchase more shares when prices are at a low level and less when prices are high. In this way, you build up your portfolio slowly but surely, getting good value for money along the way.

The logic behind dollar-cost averaging is compelling but straightforward.

- Firstly, it is a disciplined investment regimen.
- Secondly, it serves to average out the cost of the shares you buy, even if the share price fluctuates.

This process frees you from having to worry about getting your market timing right. All you need do is decide how much you are going to invest on a weekly, monthly, semiannual, and annual basis. You keep building up your portfolio.

4. MANAGE RISK THROUGH DIVERSIFICATION

Ordinarily owning shares in just one or two companies is not the best way to invest – this concentration exposes you by having all your eggs in one or too few a basket, thereby exposing you to more risk. Diversification implies reducing your risk while at the same time, maintaining an acceptable level of return. By spreading your investment across a range of markets and companies, you are reducing your exposure to the peculiarities that affect them. As a rule, the higher the degree of diversification the more you reduce your risk

Within a share portfolio, you should consider diversifying by choosing shares from different sectors within the market. You may try investing in the following industries:

- Banking
- Insurance
- Building and construction
- Health
- Agriculture

Sectors to diversify into are by no way limited to the above listed because as more industries attain market efficiency in Nigeria, and they will provide new diversification opportunities.

Within each sector, you may further diversify by investing in several other company's and not just one.

5. GET STARTED NOW

There is no apparent time to start your investment journey than to do so now. Procrastination, as it is said, is a thief of time, do away with procrastination. Excuses are cheap by the dozen. **START NOW!** Do not start the day after tomorrow, not next month, or next year, **START INVESTING NOW.**

Individuals that make money are not afraid to make decisions. No one ever earned or became wealthy by doing nothing. Financial wealth is generated by engaging in economic activities, so start now.

INVESTMENT TIP 10: Beware of INFLATION!
Whatever roles we play in the cycle of production.
We must become conscious of the eroding effect
rising prices have on our purchasing power and the
value of your money by taking up investing in shares
over the long-term beats inflationary trends.

CHAPTER 11: GLOBAL STOCKS & SHARES

Globally there are a plethora of share markets from Angola to Argentina, from Russia to France to Tokyo and from Nigeria to India to Mexico. With this sort of market span investment opportunities become staggering when viewed globally.

Your home country share market accounts for just a fraction of the world's share markets. So, if you only invest in companies listed on the local share market, you reduce your opportunity to participate in such high growth regions like China, South-East Asia, and Africa.

Further to this, some of the world's renowned companies and lucrative industries are only available in the markets of G7 countries. Massive pharmaceutical industries, car manufacturing, and financial services powerhouses may not be listed on your nation's exchange.

It is essential to note that the share markets of the world do not behave and perform similarly at the same time when compared among themselves. Some may record losses while others record gains in the same period or year. Given this knowledge, International share investment provides an opportunity for diversification and broadening your investment choices.

It is generally believed that investing in shares internationally is risky; this may not necessarily be the case as the level of risk in international investment depends on which overseas share market you invest. Some indeed carry more risk than others as they are given to more volatility and carry a lot of political and economic uncertainty while others do not.

The share market of developing economies, such as that of Nigeria, carries more risk. However, this, at the same time, brings more rewards. That is to say that they have the potential for the most price swings, implying that while prone to plunging prices, they also tend to generate the highest levels of growth much more than many markets in the world over the very long term.

The mainstream markets of western Europe, North America, and Japan tend to have lower rates of growth, but also less likelihood of drama prone downturns than the emerging markets

HOW DO I INVEST OVERSEAS?

For many people, direct investment in overseas share markets appears difficult. However, the information and technological age have made it easier to buy and sell international shares directly. One can now research markets and sectors to invest in abroad. You could have research sent to you from around the world, and access charts of thousands of companies worldwide from your home computers.

Furthermore, an increasing number of brokers such as Merrill Lynch offer international investing options and provide services to investors to trade directly in certain overseas shares (majorly American). For global shares not offered by specialist brokers, you can always appoint an overseas broker. But, remember to ensure you do your homework thoroughly before exploring this route. Also, bear in mind that regulation for opening stockbroking account will vary from one country to the next, and brokerage fees will also differ.

SHARES DYMISTIFIED – SHARES ARE NOT A MYSTERY

I stand convinced about shares as we journey into the future, for they are no mystery – they are in all simplicity part ownership of a business. Businesses are a central focus point in all economies of the world because they provide; jobs, goods, and services and reward shareholders with a share of their profits through dividends. The giving out of bonuses and dividends, in my opinion, epitomizes a fundamental and fair mechanism for the equitable distribution of wealth.

As the global population continually grows and more and more countries embrace models of capitalism, the necessity for goods and services will continue on the path of growth, and it is businesses that will supply the required products and services.

I am not convinced that there are many reasons why shares will not continue to generate significant returns above inflation to the mid or long-term investor.

Having said this, do not be lulled into a sense of comfort about the limited potential for significant downturns that may occur due to political and economic headwinds. Every couple of decades, we have experienced significant falls in prices, but what history has shown us is that the market always recovers, with the same cycles happening with overseas markets.

CONCLUSION

Some investment experts may make investing in shares sound complicated but do ensure that you remember these basics. **SHARES SECURE PART OWNERSHIP RIGHTS IN A BUSINESS ENTITLING YOU TO A SHARE OF PROFITS.** The world's population is steadily growing. Demand for both goods and services is on the increase; hence businesses will continue to come into existence and grow in size and value. Some will perform above the average, and others will fail, so endeavor to hold several shares in different companies that you are convinced will be among those that will continue as going concerns and count among the successful companies helping to minimize the risk of losing capital.

Buy quality shares when you can and hold onto them without allowing popular market sentiment or rumors to drive your actions, and you are undoubtedly on your way to building yourself genuine wealth.

It is as simple as this.

RECOMMENDATIONS FOR FURTHER READING:

On my journey to acquire financial wealth, I have found the following books of immense value. These books have, in no small way, helped to shut out distracting noise and advice from those who claim to be market wizards and analysts. Above this, they enabled me to listen to my inner voice, for no one can precisely say which way the price of a share will go. You alone are responsible for your choices and the gains or losses for investing in the market.

I hope that you do take out time to source and read these books

- **Reminiscences of a Stock Operator - by Edwin Lefevre**; this book is a classic for most traders as it illustrates the emotional highs and lows, the learning process, and hard knocks that come with venturing into the terrain that comes with stock market trading. For me, it taught me to control my emotions and feelings when dealing with the rise and falls, and the euphoria of gaining and losing.

- **The Intelligent Investor by Benjamin Graham**, widely read by investors, it opened my mind to risk-free investing and further led me to appreciate the counterbalancing risk of proper portfolio management between shares and fixed income investing (not covered in this book).

- **The Richest Man in Babylon (George S. Clawson)**, everyone appreciates an elucidating story. If ever there was a book that made me understand what need, opportunity, and risk in lay terms are, this book did. It is a guaranteed good read

- **How to Make Money in Stocks (William J. O'Neil)**, should you ever be looking for or in need of honing your stock picking strategies, look no further as this book (though quite technical), peels the skin off stock market trading and gives you a nearly foolproof way of picking the best stock on the stock market.

SUPPORT & ENQUIRIES

If you desire further support to commence your investment journey with stocks or to transform your investing strategies, contact us today.

To engage the Author, please call on +234 9065905636, or send an email to harding625@gmail.com or connect with us through the following social media platforms:

Facebook: www.facebook.com/hardingudoh

Twitter: @mercury625

Instagram: hardingudoh

LinkedIn: www.linkedin.com/in/hardingudoh

This book is available on www.amazon.com and other leading online bookstores

ACKNOWLEDGMENTS

As this book captures my experiences, I stand in gratitude to The Almighty for unceasing mercy and inspiration to press on in the face of daunting challenges.

It is with appreciation that I acknowledge the efforts of those without whose seeds, motivation, encouragement, and input this book would not have come to be.

To; mother for sowing lasting seeds thanking you on these pages is not enough, Morolayo for encouragement, know-how, and editing; Jafar, Nenpan, and DK for being my Betas.

I stand grateful.

ABOUT THE AUTHOR

 Harding Udoh is an economist and business management professional, possessing over fourteen years of working experience as a banker. He is presently the Lead Partner at Tiqian Ltd and has traded Stocks for well over a decade.

REFERENCES:

1. Paul Clitheroe (2002): Investing in Shares – How to avoid losses and create wealth. Penguin Group
2. William J. O'Neil (1995): How to Make Money in Stocks. McGraw Hill, Inc.
3. Benjamin Graham (1973): The Intelligent Investor. HaperCollins Publishers, Inc.

This book aims to provide general information about investing in shares. I have made an effort to ensure that the content is as informative as possible. Information in this book is in no way intended to replace or supersede independent or professional advice. Neither the author nor publishers may be held responsible for any action or claim resulting from the use of this book or any information contained in it.

www.ingramcontent.com/pod-product-compliance
Lightning Source LLC
Chambersburg PA
CBHW031223160726
47992CB00006B/2873